TODAY'S WORLD

FISH TO REPTILES

LIONEL BENDER

SHOOTING STAR PRESS

CONTENTS

How the book works

Each section of the book describes a group of related animals. Each begins with an introduction and a large diagram of a typical animal from the group. Smaller diagrams explain the heart and blood circulation, and the structure of the animal's skeleton. Other pages have diagrams and color photographs that illustrate important points discussed in the text. Throughout the book, charts provide a comparison of the forms and sizes of representative animals in a particular group. All illustrations are drawn to scale.

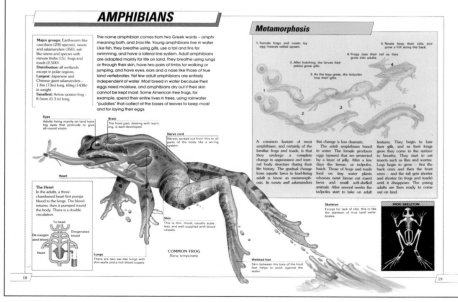

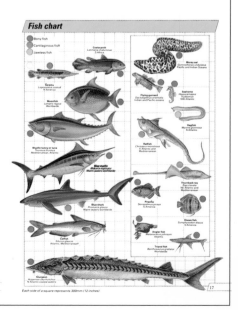

The cover photograph shows a shoal of colorful coral fish in the Red Sea.

INTRODUCTION

This book is about three major groups of animals: fish, amphibians and reptiles. In biological terms, fish are the simplest and most numerous vertebrate (backboned) animals. They were also the first vertebrates to evolve, nearly 500 million years ago. Like their invertebrate ancestors, fish spend their entire lives in water. But because nearly three-quarters of the Earth is covered with water, they have more available living space than all the other animals in the world. Fish have used this space to evolve a tremendous variety of forms, from tiny species a few millimeters long which dart among tropical coral to the enormous 18.5m (61ft) whale shark.

Amphibians, such as frogs and toads, still have to return to water to lay their eggs, but as adults most have legs and live on the land. Reptiles also lay eggs, but they are protected by a leathery shell and are laid on land. Even aquatic reptiles, such as turtles, come ashore to lay their eggs. Most walk on four legs although one large group – the snakes – have become legless and have to slither along the ground.

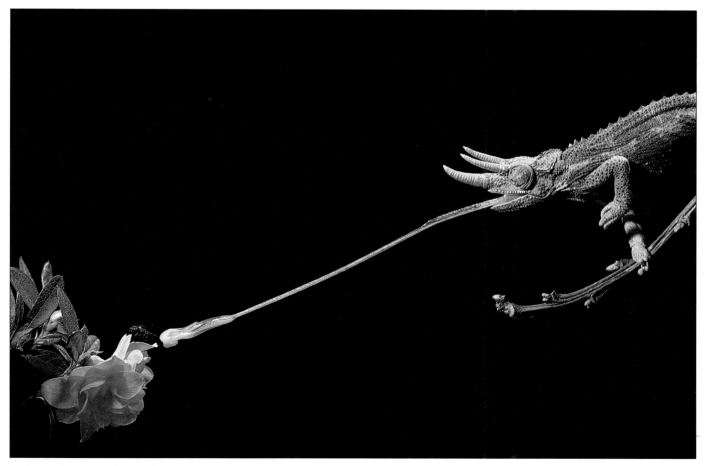

A chameleon catches a fly with its long sticky tongue.

FISH

Classification: 4 major classes – cartilaginous fish, bony fish, jawless fish and lungfish.
Commonest species: 10cm (4 in) long deep-sea bristlemouth, which preys on small crustaceans.
Rarest species: probably the coelacanth, a 2m (6ft) long offshore species, once thought to be extinct.
Lifespan: from about 6 months (small tropical species) to 85 years (sturgeon).

There are about 25,000 different species or kinds of fish, which is more than all the other backboned animals put together. They range in size from tiny gobies less than 10mm (0.4 in) long to whale sharks up to 18.5m (61 ft) in length and weighing 43 tons. All are adapted for living in the water. They are found everywhere, from the icy waters of the polar regions to tropical lakes and swamps. They are cold-blooded and breathe through gills. Most have streamlined bodies for moving quickly through the water. They use their tails to push forward and have several pairs or sets of fins to help steer and keep themselves upright.

Gills
These special breathing organs are usually protected by a tough gill-cover, the operculum.

BROWN TROUT
Salmo trutta

Brain
The areas of the brain dealing with smell and muscle control are highly developed.

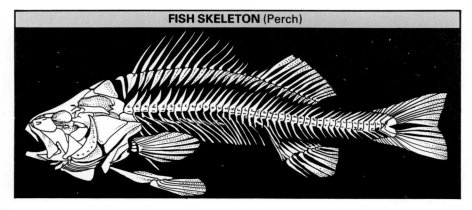

Skeleton
Most fish have a bony jointed backbone, the vertebral column, and a skull encasing the brain.

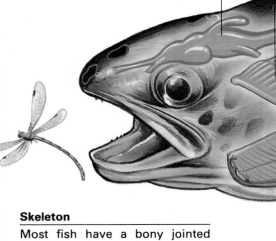

FISH SKELETON (Perch)

Heart
This muscular organ pumps blood around the animal's body. It is protected by bones that support the front fins.

Skin
The outer protective covering of most fish bears thin, overlapping tiny scales.

Blood circulation/The heart

Fish have a two-chambered heart. Deoxygenated blood (blue) is pumped around the body and chamber, the ventricle, to the gills where it is refreshed. This oxygenated blood (red) is then pumped round the body and returns to the heart's collecting chamber, the atrium, deoxygenated.

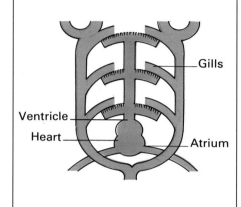

Gills
Ventricle
Heart
Atrium

Nerve cord

Protected within the backbone, the nerve cord relays messages between the brain and the rest of the body.

Breathing in water

Water out through opercular slit
Operculum
Gill filaments
Gill bars

Oxygenated blood to head and body

Water in through mouth

Gill filaments

Blood capillaries

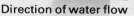

Direction of water flow

Deoxygenated blood pumped to gills by heart

In fish, sets of gills lie on each side of the head. Each gill is strengthened by a bony or gristle bar and is divided into many filaments. As the fish opens its mouth, water containing oxygen is drawn in. The water is pumped across the gills to the chamber behind the operculum. Blood flowing in capillaries within the gills is full of unwanted carbon dioxide and poor in oxygen (deoxygenated). An exchange of carbon dioxide and oxygen takes place between the deoxygenated blood and the fresh water. The gill blood becomes refreshed (oxygenated), and the water, now full of carbon dioxide, flows away as the fish closes its mouth. This water is pushed out of an opening at the back of the operculum.

SHARKS, SKATES AND RAYS

Classification: 3 main classes – sharks and dogfish (210 species), skates and rays (300 species) and chimaeras or ratfish (20 species).
Evolution: evolved some 345 million years ago from "plate-skinned" fish.
Most dangerous to people: 6m (20ft) Great White shark.

Probably the most fearsome of fish are the sharks, rays and their relatives. Most inhabit warm seas. They have skeletons made of soft cartilage or gristle instead of bone, and their skin contains small sharp scales coated with an enamel that is similar to that of human teeth. They have small gill covers and have to keep moving to circulate water over the gills in order to extract oxygen to breathe. All have a mouth adapted for biting, with a set of teeth attached to the upper and lower jaw. However, while most of these cartilaginous fish are meat-eaters, others feed on plankton, the tiny animals and plants that float in surface waters. The strange electric rays, or torpedo fish, can generate an electric current.

Feeding

The aptly named tiger shark seizes its prey.

Flesh-eating sharks mainly hunt and eat fish, but they are also scavengers and feed on dead animals. Only rarely do they attack people, and then it is usually because they have been provoked or they have smelled blood. Their teeth point backwards so that when they catch a fish it cannot escape however hard it wriggles. The two largest species, the whale shark and the basking shark, are plankton-feeders and are harmless. They have small teeth and sieve their food from the water as it is taken in through the mouth and passed to the gills. Skates and rays show similar varied feeding habits.

Swimming

A manta ray swims by flapping its "wings".

Most fish swim by producing sideways flapping movements of their body and tail. Cartilaginous fish have two sets of paired fins that extend each side of the body, and various single fins above and below the mid-line. Unlike bony fish, they do not possess an air-filled swim bladder to help stay afloat, so most species stay swimming at all times to avoid sinking. They therefore never sleep, but they do take short rest periods. Skates and rays have flatter bodies and stay near the sea bed. Their large "wings" are enlarged fins, which they use to keep stable in the water and to push themselves along.

Reproduction

Most sharks, skates and rays produce live young. Along the inner edge of the male's rear paired fins are tube-like structures, called claspers, which the male fish uses to deposit sperm inside the female. Eggs in the female are fertilized by the sperm and develop into tiny embryos. Eventually, the young fish are released into the water. Some female skates, rays and catsharks lay their eggs in horny capsules, or purses, which they deposit in sand in shallow water or attached to seaweed. This provides protection for the embryos, which take months to hatch. The empty egg cases, called mermaid's purses, can be found washed up on beaches.

Catshark embryos develop inside egg cases.

Senses

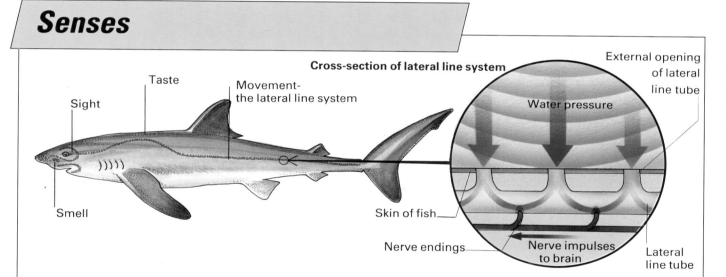

Cross-section of lateral line system

Sight
Taste
Movement-the lateral line system
Smell

External opening of lateral line tube
Water pressure
Skin of fish
Nerve endings
Nerve impulses to brain
Lateral line tube

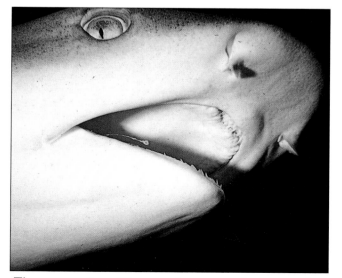
The sense of smell is more important than eyesight.

Few sharks and rays have a keen sense of vision, and most do not rely on this sense for locating food or finding their way about. All cartilaginous fish have very well-developed and sensitive senses of smell, balance and noise detection. Running along each side of the body and within the head is a network of fluid-filled tubes. This is the lateral line system which contains sense organs that are sensitive to pressure waves in the water. When the sense organs are triggered, their nerves send messages to the brain, where they are interpreted. As the fish swims along it can detect the movement of other fish and detect the difference between the motion of a healthy fish swimming nearby and the movements of an easy-to-catch injured fish struggling in the water. Their sense of smell can also detect blood in the water.

Partnerships

Remora suckerfish hitch a ride on a reef shark.

Various parasites live on the skin of fish. Other unrelated fish feed on these unwelcome animals and pieces of dead skin and are known as cleaners. The cleaners of sharks and rays are fortunate in rarely being eaten by the hosts and some, such as the remoras, who cling on using a sucker on their head, are carried around by the sharks. Pilot fish also form partnerships with sharks and rays, acting as cleaners or feeding on scraps from the shark's meal.

Weapons

Chimaeras, or ratfish, are related to sharks and rays. Like them, they have small gill covers and most live in deep oceans. They have long slender tails and at the front of their first upper fin is a poisonous sharp spine to fend off attackers.

Some rays, known as torpedo fish, have highly developed organs which can discharge a large electric current that is the same strength as household electricity supplies. They use the electric shock to stun prey.

A ratfish's poisonous spine deters attackers.

The electric ray stuns its prey using electricity.

JAWLESS FISH

Classification: one order of 50 species.
Evolution: modern representatives evolved some 270 million years ago from "shell-skinned" fish.
Common species: glutinous Atlantic hagfish and the sea lamprey.

The earliest vertebrate animals to have evolved are today represented by the hagfish and lampreys. These are generally known as jawless fish or round-mouths. They are parasites and scavengers, and instead of proper jaws have thin, horny structures surrounding a sucker-like mouth. Like eels, they do not have paired fins, and their skin is smooth, slimy and lacks scales. There are about 50 different species. Some lampreys live in the sea, others in rivers and streams, where they latch on to other fish and suck their blood, injecting a chemical that prevents blood clotting. Hagfish live in the sea, scavenging on the flesh of dead and dying fish.

Lifestyle

The primitive hagfish resembles an eel and has remained virtually unchanged from its ancestors of 500 million years ago. Hagfish live on the sea bottom, burrowing in the sand or mud during the day and scavenging for dead and dying fish or catching worms and crustaceans at night. Unlike all other fish they have no lower jaw. They use their rasp-like tongue to bore into the flesh of prey. Most species are blind and hunt by touch and smell. As adults, the jawless lampreys attach themselves to other fish, such as trout, using their sucker. They rasp away at the host's flesh with their teeth, then suck its blood. The adults breed in fresh water. The female lays the fertilized eggs in the gravel of stream- or riverbeds. Then, together with her mate, she dies. The larvae spend several years buried in river mud before finally emerging as adults. They sometimes reach plague proportions in American rivers and do great damage to fish.

An Atlantic lamprey's teeth-lined sucker mouth

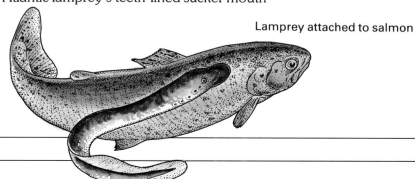

Lamprey attached to salmon

9

BONY FISH (Lakes and ponds)

Major groups: pikes, carp, sticklebacks, minnows, swamp eels, perch and lungfish.
Largest species: Nile perch — weighs up to 180kg (400lbs).
Smallest species: Dwarf pigmy goby — less than 10mm (0.4 inches) long, weight about 4mg (0.15 ounce).
Longest lived: Lake sturgeon — up to 85 years.

Fish with skeletons consisting of bone are the most numerous of all, and of these several thousand species spend their entire lives in freshwater lakes and ponds. They are able to survive in a natural world that is isolated from others and is constantly changing in temperature and nutrient levels. Some swim just below the surface, feeding on plankton or plants that grow at the water's edge. Others lurk in deep water, eating worms, insects and amphibian larvae. The most varied populations are often found in freshwater lakes or large ponds where there is plenty of food. Some pond fish grow to a very large size. Japanese golden carp, for example, weigh as much as 36kg (80 lbs).

Breeding

Most fish living in the calm waters of lakes and ponds produce eggs that remain submerged and usually attached to plants or buried in the sand or mud at the bottom. This peaceful habitat has also helped the evolution of elaborate breeding systems among fish, as in the three-spined stickleback of North America and Eurasia. The male defends a territory from other male sticklebacks, builds a nest for the eggs, attracts a female and mates with her. He flaps his fins to make the female lay eggs and then looks after the young fish.

A male stickleback stimulates a female to lay eggs.

Breathing

Many fish that live in slimy, stagnant water, or in ponds, lakes or swamps that sometimes dry out, can breathe with their gills or by gulping air into their lungs. True lungfish live in tropical swamps of Africa, Australia and South America. Some can survive total drying out. While the swamp is still damp, the fish burrows into the mud and forms a protective cocoon lined with mucus from its body. Obtaining air through tiny holes in the lid of the burrow and living on reserves of fat, it can survive until the next rainy season.

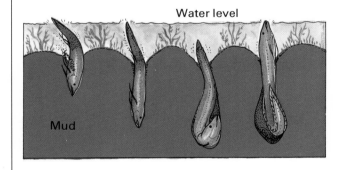

Water level

Mud

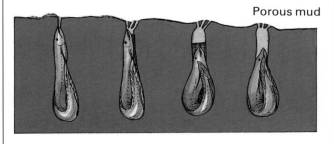

Porous mud

Food chains

The number and types of fish that live in a lake or pond largely depend on the food available and predators present. A diagram showing what eats what is known as a food web. For a fresh-water habitat such as a temperate lake, the web shows that some fish depend on plankton and invertebrates for their meals, and others on fish relatives. Such a food web starts with detritus and phytoplankton. Detritus consists of the re-mains of dead animals and plants, which sink to the bottom of the lake and form a sludge. It is grazed upon by insect larvae. The phytoplankton are eaten by tiny animals, the zooplankton, and by larger plant-feeders such as sticklebacks and carp. These are prey for meat-eaters such as pike and perch. The predatory fish may, in turn, be-come prey for fish-eating birds and mammals, such as herons, ospreys, mink and otters.

Carp feed on insect larvae and small plants.

A pike making a meal of a stickleback.

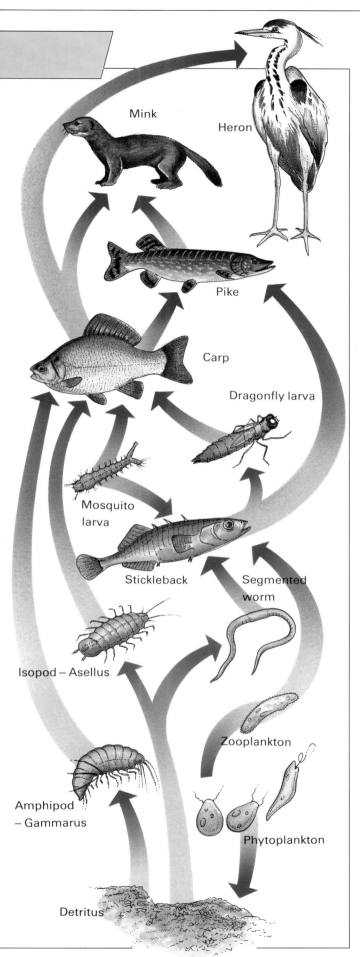

Mink

Heron

Pike

Carp

Dragonfly larva

Mosquito larva

Stickleback

Segmented worm

Isopod – Asellus

Zooplankton

Amphipod – Gammarus

Phytoplankton

Detritus

BONY FISH (Rivers and estuaries)

Major groups:
Salmon and pike (180 species), catfish (2,000), bichir and sturgeon (25), gars (7), eels (300), perch and allies (1,000), lampreys (30), mudskippers (30).

Unusual species:
Burbot, a freshwater type of cod, produces more than 1 million eggs.
Cave characin, of South America, is completely blind.

The strength of the current in a stretch of river determines the wildlife that can live there. In fast-flowing streams the only fish are strong swimmers, such as salmon and trout, or those that have suckers and can cling to rocks (for example, the sucker fish of Southeast Asia). Downstream live fish that feed on the plants, larvae and worms in silt on the riverbed. Where the current is weak, aquatic vegetation is usually rich. Here live deep-bodied fish that can weave between plants. The vegetation also provides cover for meat-eating fish that pounce on prey as it swims past. In estuaries at high tide, some sea fish swim upstream to feed in a layer of denser sea water near the bottom.

Life cycle – Atlantic salmon

Several species of fish spend their adult lives at sea but return to fresh water to breed. Among these are the salmon, ayu, and sea lamprey. Other fish live as adults in rivers and swim to the sea to breed. Famous among these are European and American eels.

Adult Atlantic salmon breed in the same river or stream where they were hatched, which they find using their sensitive sense of smell. The female lays thousands of eggs, but many are eaten by eels or birds.

The young spend one to three years in fresh water, changing from alevins, to fry, and to parr. The parr then change to smolts, which migrate to the sea. Here they spend several years. When mature, they migrate back unerringly to the place where they were born, leaping up waterfalls on the way. Then, in the shallow headwaters, they mate and lay their eggs in the gravel, to hatch the following spring. Most then die.

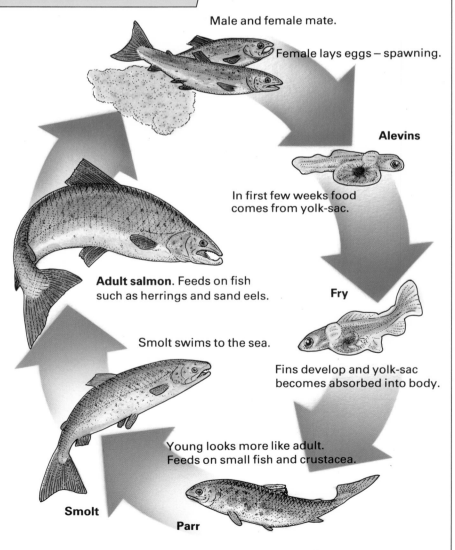

Male and female mate.

Female lays eggs – spawning.

Alevins

In first few weeks food comes from yolk-sac.

Adult salmon. Feeds on fish such as herrings and sand eels.

Fry

Smolt swims to the sea.

Fins develop and yolk-sac becomes absorbed into body.

Young looks more like adult. Feeds on small fish and crustacea.

Smolt

Parr

Out onto land

Some freshwater fish can breathe both in air and in water, and may travel across land. In autumn, when the ground is wet, adult eels migrate between rivers. They breathe through their skin, which is supplied with fine blood vessels, like a frog's skin. They also breathe aerated water carried in their gills. Adult European eels migrate thousands of miles into the mid-Atlantic to breed.

An eel photographed at night while migrating over land.

Mudskippers of Indonesia can survive on land between the tides.

Mudskippers live in mangrove swamps. They have front fins that look like short stumpy arms, which they use with their tails to skip across the mud to catch insects or to climb up the banks when the tide comes in. Before coming on land, they fill their gill chambers with water and breathe in the usual way using their gills.

Feeding

Rivers and estuaries provide fish with food such as plants and worms. Fish therefore have a variety of feeding habits — surface-feeding, stirring up creatures from the riverbed, and lurking in ambush among the plants.

Sturgeon have a small mouth to suck in snails, worms and small fish. Barbels and catfish have whisker-like sense organs around their mouth which they use to detect food. Pike have rows of sharp teeth which they use to seize other fish or even small mammals and birds at the water's edge or swimming on the surface.

The Atlantic sturgeon feeds near the riverbed.

BONY FISH (Inshore waters)

Some 15,000 species, including:
herring and anchovy (350 species); anglers and frogfish (250); cod, haddock (450); John Dory (35); scorpionfish and gurnards (1,200); mackerel, tuna and remora (6,000); flatfish (550); pufferfish (350).

The animal community of seas and oceans is supported by the phytoplankton and the seaweeds and plants that grow in coastal, or inshore, waters. Most inshore fish are those with bony skeletons. There are small herring, whiting and anchovy, which swim as shoals and that people catch for food. They rely on the safety of the shoal and on their speed and drab colors to avoid the predatory cod and tuna. Flatfish, such as plaice, have both eyes on one side of the body, which can change color to blend with a sandy or muddy sea bed and give camouflage. Scorpionfish have rows of poisonous spines, and pufferfish can inflate their bodies – adaptations that make them difficult for other fish to eat.

Shoals

Striped angel fish swim in shoals for safety.

Thousands of inshore fish, among them whiting, herring and mackerel, move and feed as a large group known as a school or shoal. They swim side by side in the same direction, turning regularly in perfect harmony. Shoal fish use their lateral line system to detect currents in the water made by their neighbors and so keep a constant distance from each other. Living and moving in a shoal gives protection by reducing the chances of a predator catching any one of them. The shoal is no defense against human fishermen, however, who sometimes scoop up a whole shoal in their nets. Around coral reefs some shoal fish are brightly colored with spots and stripes that camouflage them against the dappled sunlight reflected from the coral.

Buoyancy

Unlike cartilaginous fish, which are denser than water and tend to sink unless they keep swimming, bony fish have a swim bladder, a gas-filled sac linked to or lying close above the intestines. It maintains the buoyancy of the fish to keep it suspended in the water. The sac is filled with air taken in through the mouth, or with nitrogen and oxygen passed from the blood system. Gas is let out of the sac through a valve opening to the water, or is returned to the blood. Some predatory fish use their buoyancy to remain stationary in the water, waiting for prey to swim past.

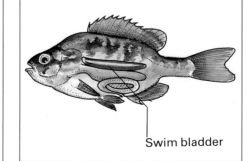

Swim bladder

Reproduction

Most sea fish produce eggs containing air sacs or oil drops, so that they float near the surface of the water. This ensures that when the young hatch they are well supplied with planktonic food. Most females lay thousands of eggs (a cod lays up to 6 million), for there is only safety in numbers. Many of the eggs are eaten by plankton-feeding fish and invertebrates, or are carried by currents to waters that are too warm or too cold for them to survive. Female seahorses, though, lay their eggs in the male's protective belly pouch. The young hatch and then stay in the pouch until they are fully developed, and when still small may swim back into the pouch for safety when danger threatens.

A male seahorse with eggs in its belly pouch

How fish swim

In swimming, a bony fish uses muscles along its body to produce a side-to-side movement of its backbone. With the help of its fins and tail, it pushes backwards and sideways against the water, steers, and stops itself dipping and rising. Using the fins on its back and underside, it steers a fairly straight course and avoids wobbling from side to side or up and down.

Flying fish can leap out of the water and glide for several meters by spreading their wing-like front paired fins. Eels, with long fins above and below, move rather like a snake.

Four-winged flying fish leap out of the waters of the Red Sea.

⬛ Thrust of tail   ⬛ Thrust of water

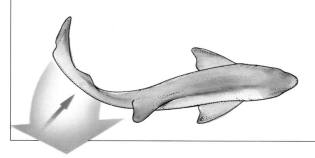

BONY FISH (Deep water)

About 2,500 species, including: spiny eels (20 species); lantern fish (300); angler fish (150); ribbon fish (50).
Longest: oarfish – up to 15m (49 ft).
Smallest: hatchet fish – 2cm (0.8 in).
Deepest living: Brotulid fish – 10,900m (36,000 ft).

In many places, oceans reach a depth of more than 10km (6 miles). But even at 1km (0.6 miles), there is no light and therefore no plants. The only food available is the rain of dead organisms from above, together with the fish and invertebrates that feed on this detritus. Yet many bony fish live there. Most are small and darkly colored. Some, such as gulper eels, have a huge mouth which they keep open at all times to catch food. Most of those that feed on the ocean floor have a downward-pointing mouth and long snout. Some have luminous organs, to attract mates or lure prey. Most remain in the ocean depths, although the 15m (49-foot) eel-like oarfish sometimes rises to the surface.

Light organs

Many free-swimming deep-sea fish possess a light organ. This is a specialized part of the body, usually near the head, that glows in the dark. Its luminous glare is used to attract prey but may also serve to deter predators or help adult males and females of a species find each other to breed. Deep-sea angler fish, which live at depths of 1,000 to 3,500m (3,300 – 11,500 ft), use their light organ as a bait to tempt inquisitive smaller fish to within reach of their huge jaws.

The light organ of a deep-sea fish glows in the dark.

Feeding

Lantern fish are deep-sea inhabitants, spending the day at depths of more than 1,000m (3,300 ft). However, at night they swim towards the surface to feed on plankton animals. The lantern fish are in turn the food of species such as viper fish and black swallowers, which have vicious pointed teeth and expandable stomachs that allow them to gulp down fish twice their size. But with food being so scarce, even a small meal may have to last them several days.

An angler fish has a luminous lure on its head.

Fish chart

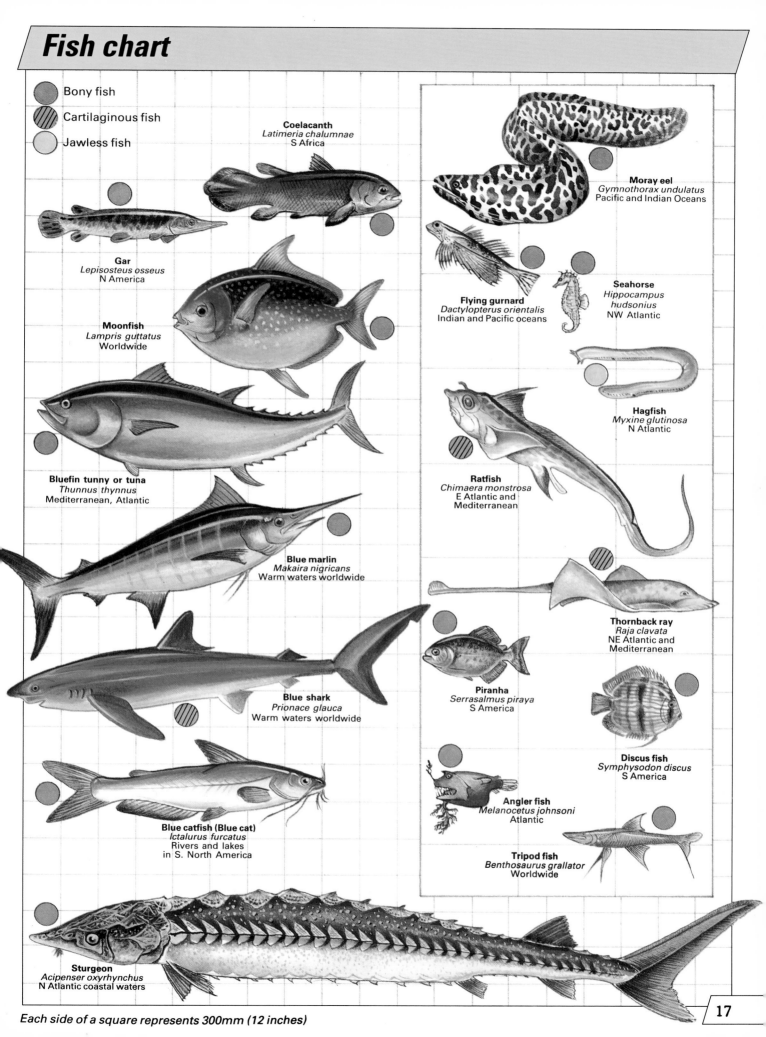

- Bony fish
- Cartilaginous fish
- Jawless fish

Coelacanth
Latimeria chalumnae
S Africa

Moray eel
Gymnothorax undulatus
Pacific and Indian Oceans

Gar
Lepisosteus osseus
N America

Flying gurnard
Dactylopterus orientalis
Indian and Pacific oceans

Seahorse
Hippocampus hudsonius
NW Atlantic

Moonfish
Lampris guttatus
Worldwide

Hagfish
Myxine glutinosa
N Atlantic

Bluefin tunny or tuna
Thunnus thynnus
Mediterranean, Atlantic

Ratfish
Chimaera monstrosa
E Atlantic and
Mediterranean

Blue marlin
Makaira nigricans
Warm waters worldwide

Thornback ray
Raja clavata
NE Atlantic and
Mediterranean

Blue shark
Prionace glauca
Warm waters worldwide

Piranha
Serrasalmus piraya
S America

Discus fish
Symphysodon discus
S America

Blue catfish (Blue cat)
Ictalurus furcatus
Rivers and lakes
in S. North America

Angler fish
Melanocetus johnsoni
Atlantic

Tripod fish
Benthosaurus grallator
Worldwide

Sturgeon
Acipenser oxyrhynchus
N Atlantic coastal waters

Each side of a square represents 300mm (12 inches)

AMPHIBIANS

Major groups: earthworm-like caecilians (150 species), newts and salamanders (350), eel-like sirens and species with minute limbs (4), frogs and toads (2,700).
Distribution: all wetlands except in polar regions.
Largest: Japanese and Chinese giant salamanders – 1.8m (6ft) long, 65kg (143lb) in weight.
Smallest: Arrow-poison frog – 8.5mm (0.3 in) long.

The name amphibian comes from two Greek words – *amphi* meaning both, and *bios* life. Young amphibians live in water. Like fish, they breathe using gills, use a tail and fins for swimming, and have a lateral line system. Adult amphibians are adapted mainly for life on land. They breathe using lungs or through their skin, have two pairs of limbs for walking or jumping, and have eyes, ears and a nose like those of true land vertebrates. Yet few adult amphibians are entirely independent of water. Most breed in water because their eggs need moisture, and amphibians dry out if their skin cannot be kept moist. Some American tree frogs, for example, spend their entire lives in trees, using rainwater "puddles" that collect at the bases of leaves to keep moist and for laying their eggs.

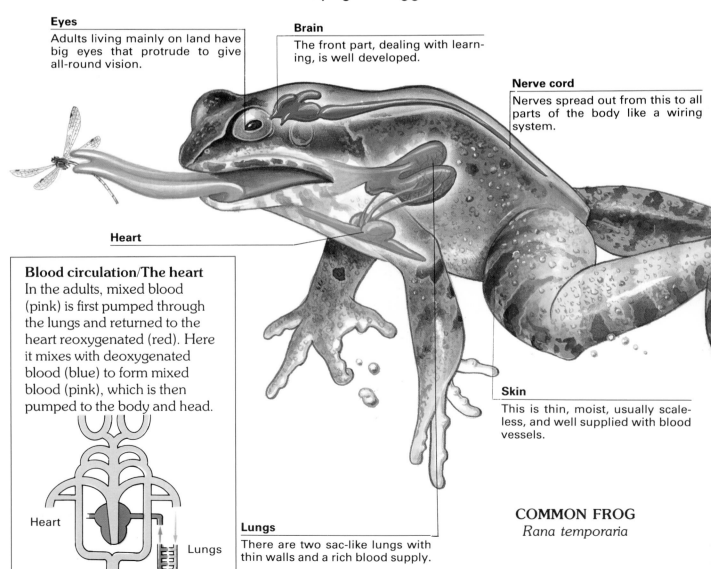

Eyes
Adults living mainly on land have big eyes that protrude to give all-round vision.

Brain
The front part, dealing with learning, is well developed.

Nerve cord
Nerves spread out from this to all parts of the body like a wiring system.

Heart

Blood circulation/The heart
In the adults, mixed blood (pink) is first pumped through the lungs and returned to the heart reoxygenated (red). Here it mixes with deoxygenated blood (blue) to form mixed blood (pink), which is then pumped to the body and head.

Heart

Lungs

Lungs
There are two sac-like lungs with thin walls and a rich blood supply.

Skin
This is thin, moist, usually scaleless, and well supplied with blood vessels.

COMMON FROG
Rana temporaria

Metamorphosis

1. Female frogs and newts lay egg masses called spawn.

2. After hatching, the larvae (tadpoles) grow gills.

3. As the legs grow, the tadpoles lose their gills.

4. Frogs lose their tail as they grow into adults.

5. Newts keep their tails and some species grow a frill along the back.

Frog

Newt

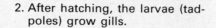

A common feature of most amphibians, and certainly of the familiar frogs and toads, is that they undergo a complete change in appearance and internal body structure during their life history. The gradual change from aquatic larva to land-living adult is known as metamorphosis. In newts and salamanders this change is less dramatic.

The adult amphibians breed in water. The female produces eggs (spawn) that are protected by a layer of jelly. After a few days to several weeks the larvae, or tadpoles, hatch. Those of frogs and toads feed on tiny water plants, whereas newt larvae eat insect larvae and small soft-shelled animals. Then, the tadpoles start to take on adult features. They begin to lose their gills, and as their lungs grow they come to the surface to breathe. They start to eat insects such as flies and worms. Legs begin to grow – first the back ones and then the front ones – and the tail gets shorter and shorter (in frogs and toads) until it disappears. The young adults are then ready to come out on land.

Skeleton

Except for lack of ribs, this is like the skeleton of true land vertebrates.

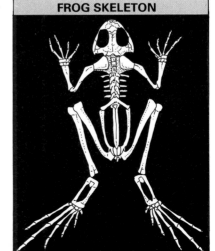

FROG SKELETON

Webbed feet

Skin between the toes of the hind feet helps to push against the water.

Living on land

Frogs and toads have powerful muscles in their hind legs, which they use to jump from place to place, although some toads generally crawl. Some species have adhesive pads and hand-like front feet that allow them to climb. Newts and salamanders raise their bodies off the ground and walk on all fours when they are on land. Limbless caecilians move like earth-worms. Sirens and amphiuma have minute legs, are mostly aquatic and swim like eels.

The fire salamander walks like a lizard.

Feeding

All adult amphibians are carnivorous. They have large mouths that can hold prey intact and still alive. Their jaws are strong, and in most newts and salamanders, bear upper and lower sets of teeth. Many species have tongues that can shoot out to capture prey. The diet of amphibians includes spiders, insects, worms, fish, reptiles, and mice and other small mammals. Some toads have a poisonous slime on their skin, which stops them from being eaten.

The Alpine newt feeds mainly on worms.

Breeding

The adults cannot breed until they are a few years old. At mating time, male newts and salamanders often acquire bright and showy colors, crests and tail membranes. These are used in courtship displays. Most male frogs and toads attract females using their voice — their croaks are mating calls. Mating takes place in the water. Often large numbers of adults group together in ponds to breed. In some species, the male produces a mass of sperm which the female takes up into her body to fertilize her eggs. In others, the female sheds the eggs into the water and the male sprays them with sperm. Females produce from a few hundred to 30,000 eggs. Many eggs are eaten by fish and other amphibia or are killed by adverse weather, so few hatch into tadpoles. Tadpoles are also a favorite prey of aquatic predators and many more are killed before maturing into adults.

Mating toads and chains of black-egged spawn

Growth

Throughout its life, the Mexican salamander, or axolotl, usually retains its gills and remains in water. Until the mid-19th century, it was believed to be a unique type of amphibian that never experienced metamorphosis. But although the axolotl looks like a larval amphibian, it can, like an adult, mate and produce offspring. It simply lacks a certain chemical, a growth hormone, that is essential for metamorphosis. If the hormone is added to the pond water in which it lives, or if the pond dries up, the axolotl loses it gills and changes to a typical adult land-living salamander. It returns to water only at mating time to lay its eggs. Cave salamanders, which live for up to ten years, spend all their time in complete darkness.

The axolotl can reproduce even at the larval stage.

Amphibians chart

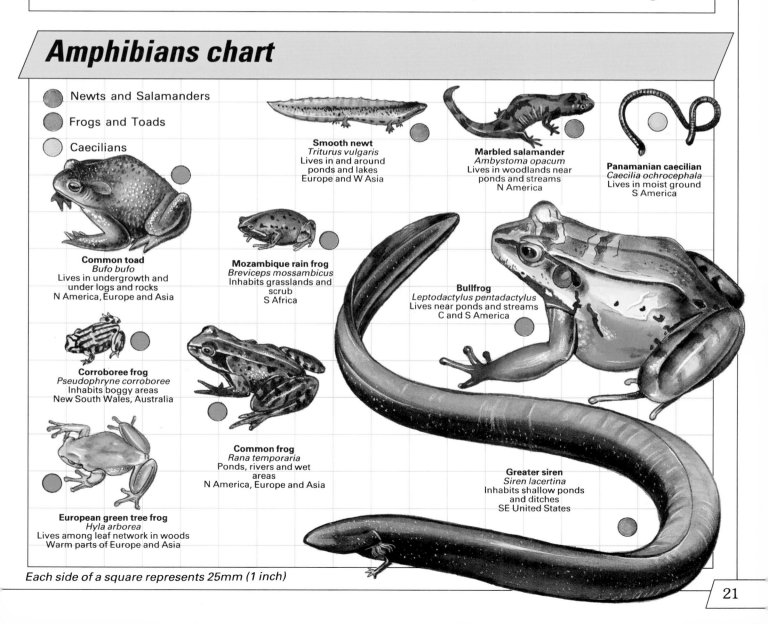

- Newts and Salamanders
- Frogs and Toads
- Caecilians

Smooth newt
Triturus vulgaris
Lives in and around
ponds and lakes
Europe and W Asia

Marbled salamander
Ambystoma opacum
Lives in woodlands near
ponds and streams
N America

Panamanian caecilian
Caecilia ochrocephala
Lives in moist ground
S America

Common toad
Bufo bufo
Lives in undergrowth and
under logs and rocks
N America, Europe and Asia

Mozambique rain frog
Breviceps mossambicus
Inhabits grasslands and
scrub
S Africa

Bullfrog
Leptodactylus pentadactylus
Lives near ponds and streams
C and S America

Corroboree frog
Pseudophryne corroboree
Inhabits boggy areas
New South Wales, Australia

Common frog
Rana temporaria
Ponds, rivers and wet
areas
N America, Europe and Asia

Greater siren
Siren lacertina
Inhabits shallow ponds
and ditches
SE United States

European green tree frog
Hyla arborea
Lives among leaf network in woods
Warm parts of Europe and Asia

Each side of a square represents 25mm (1 inch)

REPTILES

Major groups: turtles and tortoises (250 species), lizards and snakes (6,000), crocodiles and alligators (25). Extinct groups include dinosaurs.
Distribution: worldwide except polar regions.
Largest: Estuarine crocodile of Australasia, southeastern Asia – weight 2 tons, length 8.6m (28.3 ft).
Smallest: A gecko, found only in the British Virgin Islands – 18mm (0.7in).

Reptiles are the most advanced of all cold-blooded vertebrates. They are adapted best to living on land, although many species, such as turtles and crocodiles, spend most of the time in water. Reptiles breathe air using lungs, have a thick leathery skin that stops their body from drying up in hot weather, and most lay eggs that have a hard shell or tough leathery skin to protect the embryo. Unlike amphibians, reptiles do not have an aquatic larval stage. The newborn are miniature versions of the adults. Reptiles evolved from early amphibians about 300 million years ago. Some, like the dinosaurs, grew to enormous sizes. Others were ancestors of birds and mammals.

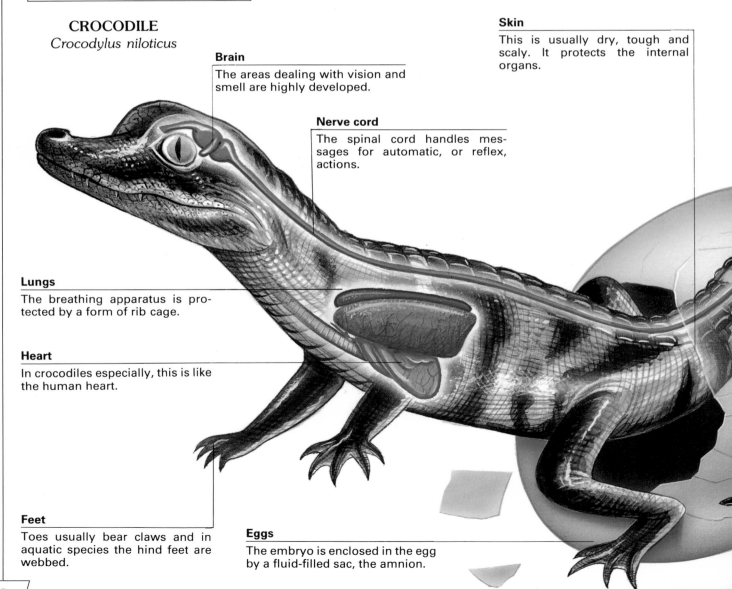

CROCODILE
Crocodylus niloticus

Brain
The areas dealing with vision and smell are highly developed.

Skin
This is usually dry, tough and scaly. It protects the internal organs.

Nerve cord
The spinal cord handles messages for automatic, or reflex, actions.

Lungs
The breathing apparatus is protected by a form of rib cage.

Heart
In crocodiles especially, this is like the human heart.

Feet
Toes usually bear claws and in aquatic species the hind feet are webbed.

Eggs
The embryo is enclosed in the egg by a fluid-filled sac, the amnion.

Blood circulation/The heart

The heart has three main chambers. The left atrium collects deoxygenated blood (blue) from the body. This is pumped by the ventricle through the lungs and returns via the right atrium. The ventricle then pumps this oxygenated blood (red) through to the head and body.

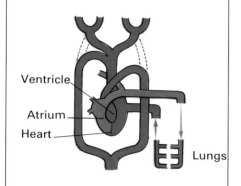

Ventricle

Atrium

Heart

Lungs

Skeleton

There are three regions: the skull and neck, backbone and limbs, and tail.

Cold-blooded

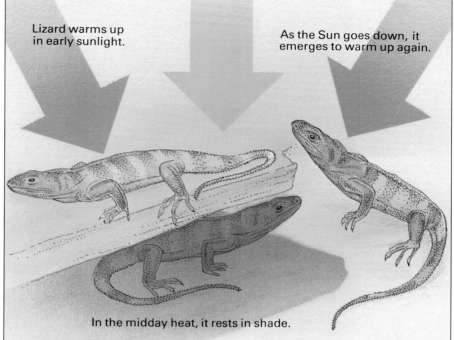

Lizard warms up in early sunlight.

As the Sun goes down, it emerges to warm up again.

In the midday heat, it rests in shade.

When the weather turns cold, reptiles become sleepy and unable to move about with their usual speed as their heartbeat and rate of breathing slow down. When it is very hot, they must shelter from the Sun's rays. This is because they are cold-blooded, which means they have no internal mechanism to regulate their body temperature. Their blood acquires the temperature of their surroundings. Reptiles are generally most active at a blood temperature in the narrow range of 30-35°C (86-97°F). They tend to alternate bouts of great activity with long periods of rest. When active, or as they bask in the Sun, their temperature rises. As it increases well above normal, they stop moving or rest in shade, slink into water, or burrow into the ground. Blood temperature then falls. For this reason, most reptiles live in warm climates, but even there few of them are active at night when it is cool unless, like crocodiles, they hunt in the water.

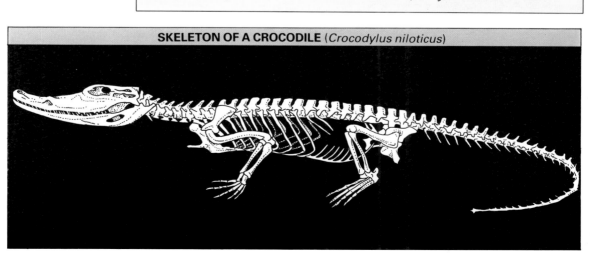

SKELETON OF A CROCODILE (*Crocodylus niloticus*)

CROCODILES AND ALLIGATORS

The crocodile family includes true crocodiles (about 15 species: common in Africa, S. America, S. Asia, Australasia), alligators and caiman (9 species: N. and S. America, China), gharial or gavial (1 species: India, Bangladesh and Pakistan).
Lifespan: 40+ years.

The closest living relatives of dinosaurs and the largest of living reptiles are members of the crocodile family (alligators and crocodiles). They have evolved for life in water and inhabit swamps and rivers in warm areas of the world. They have powerful jaws lined with sharp teeth, and once the jaws close on a prey it never escapes. All have a heavy body and an armor of bony scales. The tail is long and flattened like a paddle. Used with a whip-like action, it allows efficient swimming. On land, crocodiles are generally slow movers but can run fast. They slither along on their stomachs or raise their bodies off the ground and waddle. Crocodiles lay white eggs in the ground.

Feeding

Crocodiles are meat-eaters. They hunt mainly birds and fish. Once the prey is caught, it is dragged into the water, drowned, then eaten straight away or left to rot before being eaten. Gharials eat only fish. Some crocodiles will attack humans. All crocodiles have pointed teeth de-signed for catching and holding prey. The main differences between members of the family are the number of teeth, length and width of head, and in true crocodiles the fourth lower tooth is visible when the mouth is closed. In alligators and caimans the upper teeth are more prominent.

An American alligator attacks a young egret.

Alligator

Caiman

Crocodile

Gharial

Breathing

Living in water requires special adaptations for breathing air. Crocodiles have eyes, ears and nostrils on top of their head and snout so that they can see, hear and breathe when almost completely submerged. When under water, the windpipe, ears and nostrils can be closed with special flaps so that the mouth can be kept open to feed. The animals swim with eyelids open, but under water the eyes are covered by a transparent membrane so that the animals can still see their prey. Other aquatic reptiles, like turtles, can absorb oxygen from water taken into their body, and stay submerged for several hours at a time. They always return to the surface to breathe.

A submerged crocodile with only its eyes and nostrils showing.

Growth

Mother crocodiles lay up to 50 eggs and guard their nest until the young hatch out but do not usually care for the newborn, although they may carry the baby crocodiles carefully in their jaws and put them in a safe place. Many of the emerging crocodiles fall prey to birds, mammals and other reptiles. The newborn are miniature adults. They can immediately walk, swim and catch their own food. They grow rapidly at first. Some alligators increase in length by 30cm (12in) a year for the first few years of their life, growing eventually to a length of 5m (16 feet) or more. Most crocodiles and alligators reach sexual maturity when about eight years old.

A young alligator is safe sitting on its mother's head.

LIZARDS

Major types: Geckos (700 species), iguanas (630), agamids (300), chameleons (90), skinks (600), African and Eurasian lizards (150), South American lizards (200), slow-worms (75), worm lizards (120), monitors (25).
Related to and resembling lizards is the tuatara of New Zealand, which has a strange third eye on top of its head.

Ranging from the aggressive 3m (10ft) long Komodo dragon of Indonesia to the small harmless green lizards and wall lizards familiar in temperate areas, these reptiles are highly successful. They have adapted to many different lifestyles. The North American Gila monsters and beaded lizards have a poisonous bite and prey on small rodents. Worm lizards, slow-worms and some skinks have no limbs. They may burrow underground to feed on earthworms and slugs. Geckos are mostly nocturnal and climb trees to prey on insects. Flying dragons have a membrane of skin between their toes, which they spread out so that they can glide between the trees in which they live.

Self-defense

The green coloration common in tree-living lizards and the patchy colors of lizards that scurry around in dry grass or climb over walls act as camouflage. Chameleons can change their colors to merge with their surroundings, although this may be to give them a chance to attack prey rather than for self-defense. Other lizards, such as the thorny devils and girdled lizards, have weapons such as facial, body or tail spikes. They use these to warn off would-be attackers. Frilled lizards use a display of force and terror to defend themselves. They spread out a frill around their necks, open their brightly colored mouths, and in this way look much more aggressive than they really are.

Many lizards shed their tail when attacked and later grow a new one. Their enemy is fooled by the decoy. In chameleons, color changes of the skin are produced by special cells known as chromatophores. These contain granules of several colored pigments. Depending on messages received from the brain via the spinal cord, the cells are made to expand or contract in the desired way.

A frilled lizard stands and faces an attacker.

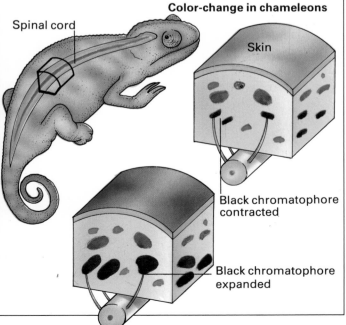
Color-change in chameleons
Spinal cord
Skin
Black chromatophore contracted
Black chromatophore expanded

Feeding

Lizards' food consists mainly of insects such as flies, ants, termites and grasshoppers. Some species supplement this diet with worms, snails, birds' eggs, small rodents and other mammals, and even fruit and other reptiles. Lizards generally swallow their prey whole. They grasp the food in their jaws then gobble it up in a series of snatching movements of the mouth. When catching insects in particular, many lizards use their tongue as a hunting weapon. Chameleons, for example, have a sticky tongue almost as long as their body and tail which they shoot out at lightning speed and with amazing accuracy to catch their prey. They then pull the tongue back into the mouth together with their meal stuck to the end. In this manner, they can sometimes successfully catch even birds. Each eye can move independently, giving them a wide field of vision and allowing them to judge distance very accurately. A prehensile tail serves as a fifth limb.

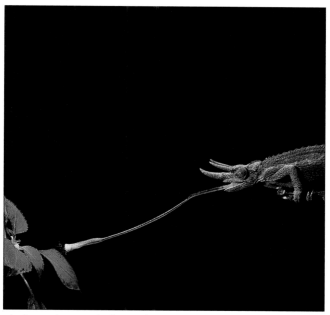
A three-horned chameleon catches a fly.

Movement

Most lizards have four legs and can walk and run. They differ from mammals in having legs that stick out on each side of the body rather than under it. They usually move slowly forward on their stomachs, waving their bodies side to side to push themselves along. Desert lizards, such as the African gridiron-tailed lizard, can run along on just two legs. They lift their heads and stomachs off the ground, rear up on their hind legs, and scurry along. Their long tails act as a counter-balance. Some lizards are adept at climbing. Limbless lizards, for example skinks, slow-worms and other burrowing species, resemble and move like snakes.

The basilisk lizard can run across a pond's surface.

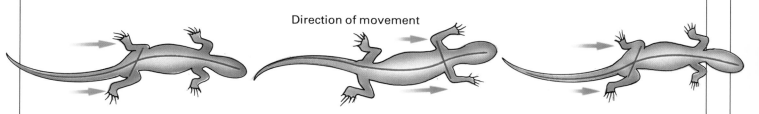
Direction of movement

Hind limbs push hard against ground   Front limbs pull body forward   Hind limbs exert force again

TORTOISES AND TURTLES

Major groups: Snapper and mud turtles (25 species), tortoises and freshwater turtles (115), leathery turtle (1), marine turtles (5), side-necked turtles (45).
Largest: Pacific leatherback turtle – 2.2m (7 ft) long, weighing 500kg (1200 lb).
Longest lived: Seychelles Marion's tortoise – 155 years.
Slowest moving: Seychelles giant tortoise – 0.37 kph (0.23 mph).

With a body surrounded by a protective shell, these are the oldest group of reptiles, and have hardly changed in 200 million years. There are three main groups. Tortoises live on land, have a domed shell, stumpy legs and feed mostly on plants. Their relatives, freshwater turtles, live in rivers and lakes. They are plant- and meat-eaters. The second group, turtles, comprises mostly marine creatures. Their shell is flatter and they have paddle-shaped feet used for swimming. The third group, side-necked turtles and their allies, live in fresh water but tuck their heads under the edge of the shell instead of pulling it in. All aquatic species come to the surface of the water to gulp air into their lungs. Also, although they may mate in the water, females of aquatic species come ashore to lay their eggs in a hollow in the ground. They then return to the water, leaving the eggs to hatch on their own.

Life cycle

Among tortoises and turtles, the breeding season begins with males approaching females. Mating may last hours, and because of the animals' shells, males often have to stand almost upright to fertilize the eggs successfully. Mother tortoises lay their eggs in a shallow depression or natural hole in the ground and leave them to hatch in the sun. Female marine turtles lay their eggs in holes dug on sandy beaches and cover them with sand. This serves to hide the eggs from predators such as sea-birds, and to keep them warm. Days or weeks later the young hatch out. They must struggle to the surface and make their way as fast as they can to the sea. Many are caught and eaten by crabs, snakes and birds. With turtles, adulthood is reached between 12-15 years, and they are among the longest-lived animals. Giant tortoises of the Galapagos Islands, for example, are known to live for more than a hundred years.

A leathery turtle scrapes a hole for its eggs.

Newly hatched leathery turtles scuttle to the sea.

Shells

The shell, or carapace, is composed of bony plates covered by horny scales. The arched upper shell is fused to the backbone and to the ribs, which thus cannot be used in breathing. Instead air is drawn into the lungs by a pumping action of body muscles. The under-shell is less heavily armored. Upper and lower shell are joined in the middle region on each side, leaving openings in front and behind for the head, legs and tail. In most species, the head can be withdrawn under the carapace. The shell of a tortoise grows throughout life, but growth stops during hibernation. As a result, the patterns on the shell have growth rings, which can be used to estimate the animal's age.

Shell shapes among tortoises of some Galapagos Islands

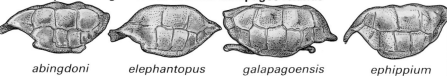

abingdoni   *elephantopus*   *galapagoensis*   *ephippium*

The giant tortoise can be identified by the shape of its shell.

Feeding

Instead of teeth, tortoises, turtles and sea turtles have a horny beak with sharp cutting edges. These beaks cannot shred or crush food. Also, their broad, fleshy tongues cannot be protruded to collect morsels of food. They are forced to seize plant or animal food in their jaws and chop it into large pieces and swallow it slowly.

A Greek tortoise feeding on lettuce leaves.

Migration

Adult marine turtles, such as the green turtle, migrate each year in great numbers from feeding areas in shallow parts of the sea to the same distant breeding ground. There they haul themselves onto land, moving clumsily up the beach, lay their eggs and bury them in the sand, then return to the sea until the next breeding season.

The green turtle swims to the shore to breed.

SNAKES

Major groups: blind snakes (275 species), burrowing shield-tailed snakes (50), constrictors (70), water snakes (2), vipers (100), cobras and sea-snakes (200), Colubrid snakes (1,500).
Longest: Reticulated python – 8.7m (28.5ft).
Most poisonous: Sea snake of N.W. Australian waters.

With their long, slender, limbless bodies, lack of eardrums, and eyelids fused to form a transparent protective covering over the eyes, present-day snakes probably evolved from lizards. Most snakes live in warm places, inhabiting deserts, tropical forests and grasslands, where they use various methods of moving along the ground. They are adapted to a life above ground, although some live in water, where they produce live young. Snakes eat live animals and the eggs of birds and other reptiles, which they usually swallow whole. They can swallow prey larger than themselves. Some species are poisonous, although most snakes are harmless to humans.

Jaws

Snakes are unique among reptiles in that they can move their upper and lower jaws apart during swallowing. Because each jaw can move independently, and with flexible elastic ligaments linking the halves of the lower jaw, snakes can open their mouth enormously wide. A large python can devour a small antelope, pig or monkey whole. To help swallow such large prey, they have evolved several features. First, they have backward pointing teeth to grip the food and pull it back into the mouth (and the front-fanged vipers and rattlesnakes can fold their fangs back out of the way when swallowing prey). Second, the whole brain is encased in bone so it cannot easily get damaged. Third, the rib cage can enlarge to allow large items to pass down the throat. Also, because snakes have no legs, they lack the bones that would form shoulder and hip girdles, which means they can consume prey wider than their bodies.

An African egg-eating snake

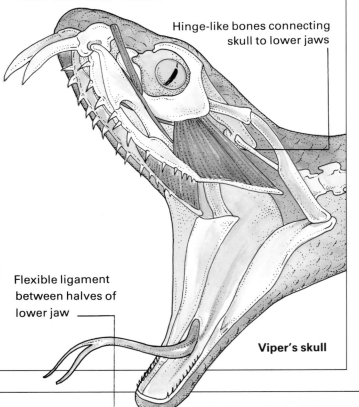
Hinge-like bones connecting skull to lower jaws

Flexible ligament between halves of lower jaw

Viper's skull

Killing and feeding

Snakes must first kill or render their prey unconscious. Boas and pythons seize the prey in their jaws, wrap themselves round it, and then stop it breathing. They are known as constrictors. Smaller snakes kill or stun their prey using venom, which is a mixture of poisons. Venom is injected through a pair of special teeth called fangs. Vipers have long front fangs that fold back when not in use. Their venom attacks the prey's blood system. Cobras have fixed short front fangs and produce a venom affecting the nervous system. Colubrids, such as the bird-eating Boomslang snake, have poisonous fangs at the back of the jaw. They attract prey by flicking out their brightly colored tongues. Grass snakes also have small fixed fangs at the back of the jaw, but do not have a bite harmful to humans.

A black-necked spitting cobra

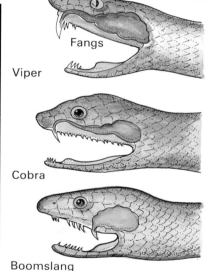

Venom sac

Fangs

Viper

Cobra

Boomslang

A python crushes a gazelle and begins to swallow it whole.

Movement

Snakes have no legs and have evolved their own way of moving on land. A snake can use its tail as a lever to push its head and trunk forwards then, with its neck, pull the rest of its body along. In serpentine motion the snake adopts a wave-like action and pushes against objects to gain leverage. In water, snakes use this action to swim, and many sea snakes have a flattened tail which acts like an oar or paddle. On loose soil or sand, snakes arch their head forwards, put it down in a sideways loop, then draw up the rest of the body. Snakes that move in this way are called sidewinders.

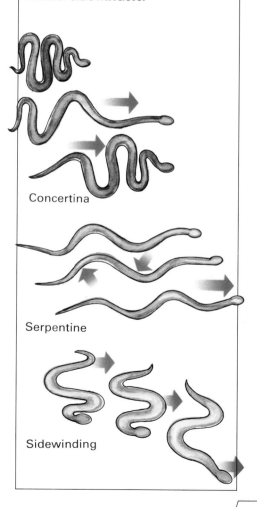

Concertina

Serpentine

Sidewinding

Mating

Male snakes often compete for or display to the females by using elaborate dances. Rival males may entwine their entire bodies in a show of strength. Males trail the females by detecting the scent of skin secretions. To mate, partners lie alongside each other, and tropical species may breed several times a year. Sea snakes usually give birth to live young but many land species lay eggs. Few tend their eggs, and the young must fend for themselves.

European adders entwined while mating

Growth

Snakes, like lizards, from time to time shed the horny layer of skin which covers their scales. This is to allow for growth. Young snakes may shed, or slough, the skin six or seven times a year. The old skin splits, usually around the lips, and the snake wriggles out, peeling it off like a glove. After sloughing the snake looks as if it has been freshly painted. A rattlesnake grows a new segment on the rattle at the end of its tail each time the skin is shed.

A Gaboon viper after shedding its skin

Senses

Vision and hearing are less highly developed than the sense of smell. Most snakes see things in only black and white, and not color. Some, especially burrowing species, are blind. Yet rattlesnakes can detect moving objects at distances of 45m (50yd). All snakes have ears that are sensitive to only low-frequency sounds. However, they seem able to detect vibrations in the ground via nerve cells around bones in the head. Their tongues are more sensitive to smell and touch. The main organ of smell, Jacobson's organ, is positioned on the roof of the animal's mouth. By flicking its tongue, a snake transfers scent particles to sensitive cells lining the organ. During swallowing, the tongue is carefully kept flat on the floor of the mouth so that it does not get injured. Some snakes, called pit vipers, can sense the body heat of warm-blooded prey such as rats, squirrels and birds using temperature sensitive pits next to their eyes. These heat-sensors work even in complete darkness.

A large-headed tree snake from Costa Rica

Reptiles chart

Gila monster
Heloderma suspectum
Mexico and S United
States

**Eastern Diamondback
rattlesnake**
Crotalus adamanteus
United States

Crocodile family

Lizards and snakes

Tortoises and turtles

Tuatara, a lizard-like
primitive reptile

Painted terrapin
Chrysemys picta
N America

Green turtle
Chelonia mydas
All warm oceans

Leopard tortoise
Geochelone pardalis
S and E Africa

Jackson's chameleon
Chameleo jacksonii
Africa

Tokay gecko
Gekko gekko
SE Asia

Frilled lizard
Chlamydosaurus kingi
Australia, New Guinea

Slow-worm
Anguis fragilis
Europe, N Africa, Asia
Minor

Tuatara
Sphenodon punctatus
Islands off New Zealand

Indian python
Python molurus
India and SE Asia

Gharial
Gavialis gangeticus
India, Pakistan and
Bangladesh

Nile crocodile
Crocodylus niloticus
Africa

King cobra
Ophiophagus hannah
SE Asia

Each side of a square represents 150mm (6 inches)

33

CLASSIFICATION CHART

There are more than a million species of animals in the world. Biologists – scientists who study living things – have divided these up into several major groups based on the similarities between them and how they are thought to have evolved. Within the Animal Kingdom, the most important division is between those animals with backbones, the vertebrates, and those without, the invertebrates. Fish, divided in turn into bony, cartilaginous and jawless types, are considered to form the link between vertebrates and invertebrates. Amphibians evolved from fish, and reptiles from amphibians. This chart shows representative species of each major division of fish, amphibians and reptiles.

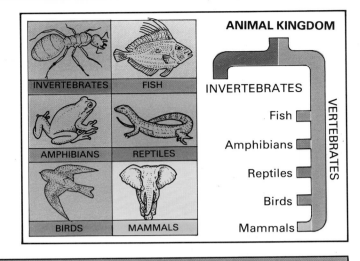

ANIMAL KINGDOM

INVERTEBRATES FISH
AMPHIBIANS REPTILES
BIRDS MAMMALS

INVERTEBRATES
Fish
Amphibians
Reptiles
Birds
Mammals
VERTEBRATES

FISH							
Bony Fish					**Cartilaginous fish**		**Jawless fish**
RAY FINNED FISH			FLESHY FINNED FISH		CHIMAERAS	SHARKS AND RAYS	
Teleosts	Gars and Bowfins	Bichirs and Sturgeons					

Tarpons — Gars — Sturgeons — Coelacanth — Chimaeras — Sharks — Hagfish and Lampreys
Bowfins — Bichirs — Lungfish — Skates and Rays
Eels
Spiny eels — Milk fish — Cod fish — Swamp eels
Herrings — Carps — Squirrel fish — Flying gurnards
Bony tongues — Catfish — Flying fish and killifish — Scorpion fish and gurnards
Mormyrids and gymnarchids — Sand rollers and pirate perches — John Dory and allies — Sea moth
Salmon and pikes — Toadfish — Moonfish — Perches
Lantern fish — Clingfish — Flatfish
Macristiid — Angler fish — Sticklebacks and seahorses — Snakeheads — Triggerfish and puffer fish

AMPHIBIANS

Caecilians — Newts, Sirens and Salamanders — Frogs and toads

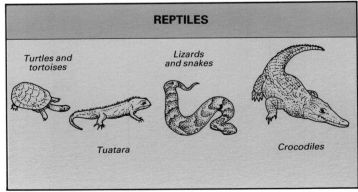

REPTILES

Turtles and tortoises — Lizards and snakes — Tuatara — Crocodiles

All groups belong to vertebrates

GLOSSARY

adaptation feature or behavior that allows an animal to live in a particular environment or feed on a specific food.

aquatic animal or plant that lives in water.

artery blood vessel that carries blood from the heart to the body tissues and organs.

bone hard material forming skeleton of most vertebrates.

brain coordination and control center of an animal's nervous system.

capillary narrow, thin-walled blood vessel that permits oxygen, carbon dioxide and food materials to pass between cells of the body and the bloodstream.

carnivore meat-eating animal.

cartilaginous fish those whose skeleton is composed of cartilage – elastic tissue.

cell building-block of all living creatures. Different types of cells have different jobs – for example, nerve, muscle, blood cells – but all work in the same way.

deoxygenated blood blood low in oxygen but high in carbon dioxide content. Carbon dioxide is a waste product of cell chemistry and must be eliminated from the body.

egg female reproductive cell with its own provision of food for the growing embryo. The egg must be fertilized by the male sperm before development of the embryo can begin.

embryo stage in development of an animal – from the fertilized egg until the young hatches or is born.

evolution very slow, probably gradual, process by which new species arise as a result of changes that occur in populations of animals or plants.

fertilization fusing together of male and female reproductive cells (sperm and egg) to form an embryo.

gills feathery breathing organs of animals that live in water – the equivalent of lungs in land-living animals.

habitat place where an animal or plant lives such as a forest, desert or sea.

heart muscular pumping organ that sends blood to all parts of the body. It may have one or two collecting chambers, or atria (singular atrium), and one or two distributing chambers, or ventricles.

herbivore animal that feeds on plant material such as seeds, leaves, fruits.

host creature on or in which a parasite lives.

invertebrate animal that lacks a backbone. Many invertebrates are aquatic creatures, including jellyfish, sponges and corals, but insects form the majority.

larva young, immature stage in the life cycle of many animals. It is usually very different in appearance from the adult and cannot reproduce.

locomotion method of movement from one place to another, such as running, swimming or jumping.

nerve cord another name for the spinal cord.

nervous system/nerves special body structure(s) able to send, receive and, as the brain, interpret information in the form of electrical messages (known as nerve impulses).

organ major part of an animal or plant which has a specific task, for instance the heart, brain, and lungs. Organs are made up of different types of tissues, which are themselves composed of various cells.

oxygenated blood blood rich in oxygen.

parasite creature that lives in or on another one from which it gets its food (the host). A parasite may eventually kill its food source.

predator animal that gets its food by hunting and killing other animals.

prehensile able to seize or grasp.

reproduction process of producing offspring. Usually involves the male fertilizing the female's egg with his sperm.

scavenger animal that eats dead or dying animals.

skull box-like skeleton of the head composed of many bones fused together and providing protection for the brain and sense organs, such as the eyes.

species animals and plants that have the same structure and that are capable of reproducing together.

spinal cord extension of the brain that runs the length of the body and is enclosed within a canal in the vertebral column, or backbone. Nerves radiate out from the spinal cord to reach all parts of the body.

vein blood vessel carrying blood from body to heart.

vertebral column another name for the backbone. It consists of many bony units linked together to form a flexible stiffening rod the length of the body.

Index

All entries in bold are found in the Glossary

Photographic Credits
l=left, r=right, t=top, b=bottom, c=center
Cover: Peter Scoones/Planet Earth; contents page and pages 10, 11 (both), 13 (t and c), 15 (both), 24, 27 (both), 29 (l), 30, 32 (r and b): Bruce Colman; pages 6 (l), 8 (t), 20 (b), 25 (both), 26, 28 (both) and 29 (t and r): Ardea; pages 6 (r) and 14: Herwarth Voightman/Planet Earth; page 7 (t): David George/Planet Earth; page 7 (b): Christian Petron/Planet Earth; pages 8 (l), 9 and 20 (l): Ken Lucas/Planet Earth; page 8 (r): Alex Double/Planet Earth; page 13 (b): Jim Greenfield/Planet Earth; page 16 (both): Peter David/Planet Earth; page 20 (r): John Lythgoe/Planet Earth; page 21: Adrian Stevens/Planet Earth; page 31 (t): NHPA; page 31 (b): Zefa; page 32 (l) and back cover: Survival Anglia.